W9-BXZ-208

SCHOLASTIC
News
Nonfiction Readers

From Eye to Potato

by Ellen Weiss

Children's Press®
A Division of Scholastic Inc.
New York Toronto London Auckland Sydney
Mexico City New Delhi Hong Kong
Danbury, Connecticut

These content vocabulary word builders are for grades 1–2.

Consultant: Pati Vitt, PhD, The Institute for Plant Conservation Biology, Chicago Botanic Garden, Glencoe, Illinois

Reading Consultant: Cecilia Minden-Cupp, PhD, Early Literacy Consultant and Author, Chapel Hill, North Carolina

Photographs © 2008: age fotostock: 7 (Banana Stock), 23 top left (Heinz Tschanz-Hofmann); Alamy Images/Keith M. Law: cover left inset, 4 bottom right, 16 bottom right, 20 bottom; Envision Stock Photography Inc.: 23 bottom right (Mark Ferri), back cover, 17 background (James Marshall); Getty Images/Eric Brasseur/Photonica: 19, 21 top; Photo Researchers, NY: cover center inset, 5 top right, 13, 21 bottom (Adam Hart-Davis), 5 top left, 17 inset (Joyce Photographics), 4 bottom left, 16 bottom left (Peter Menzel/Science Photo Library); Photolibrary/Mauritius Die Bildagentur Gmbh: cover background; StockFood, Inc.: 23 bottom left (Brauner), 23 top right (Christina Peters Photography); VEER/R. White: cover right inset, 2, 4 top, 9, 20 top, 20 right, 21 left; Visuals Unlimited: 5 bottom left, 9 inset (Wally Eberhart), 1, 11 (Kim Fennema), 5 bottom right, 15, 21 right (Dr. Kenneth Whitney).

Book Design: Simonsays Design!
Book Production: The Design Lab

Library of Congress Cataloging-in-Publication Data
Weiss, Ellen, 1949–
From eye to potato / by Ellen Weiss.
p. cm.—(Scholastic news nonfiction readers)
Includes bibliographical references and index.
ISBN-13: 978-0-531-18535-3 (lib.) 978-0-531-18788-3 (pbk.)
ISBN-10: 0-531-18535-4 (lib.) 0-531-18788-8 (pbk.)
1. Potatoes—Juvenile literature. I. Title. II. Series.
SB211.P8W326 2007
635'.21—dc22 2007004487

No part of this publication may be reproduced in whole or in part, or stored in a retrieval system, or transmitted in any form or by any means, electronic, mechanical, photocopying, recording, or otherwise, without written permission of the publisher. For information regarding permission, write to Scholastic, 557 Broadway, New York, NY 10012.

©2008 Scholastic Inc.
All rights reserved. Published in 2008 by Children's Press, an imprint of Scholastic Inc.
Published simultaneously in Canada. Printed in the United States of America. 44
SCHOLASTIC, CHILDREN'S PRESS, and associated logos are trademarks and/or registered trademarks of Scholastic Inc.
1 2 3 4 5 6 7 8 9 10 R 17 16 15 14 13 12 11 10 09 08

CONTENTS

Word Hunt 4–5

Yum! Potatoes! 6–7

Eyes Grow 8–9

Sprouts Sprout 10–11

Roots Grow Down 12–13

Tubers 14–15

Flowers and Fruits 16–17

Plant One Yourself 18–19

Potato Life Cycle 20–21

Your New Words 22

More Tubers 23

Index 24

Find Out More 24

Meet the Author 24

WORD HUNT

Look for these words as you read. They will be in **bold**.

eyes
(eyez)

seeds
(seedz)

seed potatoes
(seed puh-**tay**-tohz)

fruits
(froots)

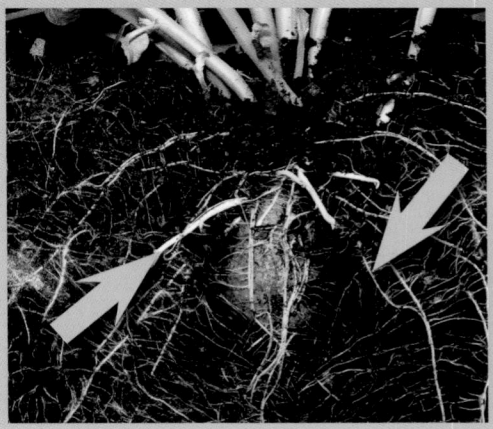

roots
(roots)

sprouts
(sprouts)

tubers
(**too**-burz)

Yum! Potatoes!

How do you like to eat your potatoes? Mashed? Baked?

People eat potatoes in many parts of the world.

Potatoes grow in many places, too.

They grow in a very interesting way.

What happens when you store a potato too long?

Little white **sprouts** start growing out of the potato.

They grow from the **eyes** of the potato.

They aren't good to eat.

But they are good for growing new potatoes!

These eyes can't see, but they can grow.
eyes
sprouts

New potato plants can grow from eyes.

The sprout is the beginning of a new plant.

It gets bigger and starts to grow leaves.

You don't need seeds to grow potato plants.

How does a sprout turn into a plant?

First, someone plants the sprouted potato in the ground.

Soon it will begin to grow **roots**.

The roots soak up water for the plant.

Roots grow down from the plant.

Plants need food to grow.

The potato provides food to get the plant started.

Later, the plant will make new food.

It will store extra food in parts called **tubers**. Tubers can be good food for people, too.

The potatoes that you eat are tubers!

Potato plants may grow flowers and **fruits**.

Potato fruits have **seeds** inside.

Farmers usually plant sprouted potatoes instead of potato seeds. They call these potatoes **seed potatoes**.

Never eat a potato fruit.
It can make you sick!

Find a potato in your kitchen.

Put it in a warm place with lots of light.

Plant it when the eyes grow sprouts.

Take good care of it.

Someday, you can eat potatoes you grow yourself.

Yum!

Dig up your potato plants to find the potatoes.

POTATO LIFE CYCLE

1

A potato begins to sprout.

2

The sprouted potato, or seed potato, is planted.

5

Dig up the potato plant when the potatoes are ready for eating!

4

Special roots called tubers store food. Potatoes are tubers.

3

The potato grows roots under the soil. The potato plant appears above the soil.

YOUR NEW WORDS

eyes (eyez) the parts of a potato from which sprouts grow

fruits (froots) the parts of flowering plants that contain seeds

roots (roots) parts of plants that grow underground and absorb water

seeds (seedz) parts of flowering plants from which a new plant can grow

seed potatoes (seed puh-**tay**-toze) sprouted potatoes that can be used to grow new potato plants

sprouts (sprouts) new plant growth

tubers (**too**-burz) thick, underground plant stems; many kinds of tubers can be eaten

cassava
(kuh-**sah**-vuh)

jicama
(**hee**-kuh-muh)

sweet potato
(sweet puh-**tay**-toh)

water chestnut
(**waw**-tur **chest**-nut)

INDEX

eating, 6, 8, 14, 18
eyes, 8, 10, 18

farmers, 16
flowers, 16
food, 14
fruits, 16

leaves, 10

planting, 12, 16, 18

roots, 12

seed potatoes, 16, 20
seeds, 16

sprouts, 8, 10, 12

tubers, 14

water, 12

FIND OUT MORE

Book:

Coy, John, and Carolyn Fisher (illustrator). *Two Old Potatoes and Me.* New York: Alfred A. Knopf, 2003.

Website:

British Potato Council
www.potatoesforschools.org.uk/

MEET THE AUTHOR

Ellen Weiss has received many awards for her books for kids. She has a garden, where she is especially good at growing weeds.